Especially for
Us
_____

From
Us
_____

Date
11 − 25 − 10
_____

Our Family Christmas

A Keepsake Devotional for the Holiday Season

KARON PHILLIPS GOODMAN

BARBOUR
PUBLISHING

Published by Barbour Publishing, Inc., P.O. Box 719, Uhrichsville, Ohio 44683
www.barbourbooks.com

Our mission is to publish and distribute inspirational products offering exceptional value and biblical encouragement to the masses.

 Member of the
Evangelical Christian
Publishers Association

Printed in China.

Contents

Introduction

"O Come, All Ye Faithful," Your Family Together...

"I believe that you are the Christ, the Son of God, who was to come into the world."
JOHN 11:27 NIV

Because Christ our Savior was born on Christmas Day, our world was forever changed. The *wondrous gift* God gave us became the source of every wondrous gift to follow, and we have the Christmas season in which to hold our family close in *comfort and joy* and inspire us throughout the year to return *our finest gifts* to Him.

The Christmas story is an old story, but its power and purity remind us of the greatest and deepest love and sacrifice of our Father. One *silent night* in a town called Bethlehem, *Christ was born of Mary*. God's gift of His everlasting love came to us in flesh and stays in Spirit, our Immanuel promise always guiding us and accepting our humble efforts to serve with Him.

When our *hearts prepare Him room*, we fear not the world we don't understand, but trust instead *the angel voices* still as true as *the night when Christ was born*. And we have the blessed opportunity to *go tell it on the mountain* in our lives to all who will hear of *Jesus, Lord at thy birth*, because the best thing to do with every priceless gift is to share it.

The sharing of the gift of Jesus begins in our homes, with those we love the most. We rejoice in the faithful reminder of His love and grace, *goodness and light*. We pause for this yearly booster shot of celebration because He is Lord of lords and King of kings, the gift we both share and receive with each breath because He lives. It's *peace on earth* to spend special moments with our family during this special season. *Let us adore Him* together.

Let us see beyond the wrapping paper and blinking lights to the everyday opportunities to bring *glory to our newborn King*, through all we say and do in kindness and generosity, faith and love. He's waiting for us to see past presents and dinners to the significance of *the first Noel*, waiting for us to live boldly the message and spirit of Christmas and do our part to deliver *goodwill to men* everywhere.

And we learn best when we're teaching those who depend on us the most. So for a few moments these next few days, in the *light of a star sweetly gleaming* and with those we love, let us remember this gift of *joy to the world*.

Do you hear what I hear? That's God's whisper of love in the gift of Christ, when *away in a manger*, dark and quiet, the *Son of God, love's pure light*, is born of Mary and given to us.

Do you see what I see? Each reading and activity here is to accompany you and your family through this blessed season. May your memories of this experience of *wondering love* return the joy of the gift of Jesus to you and your family on Christmas and always—because Christmas is a message that lasts a lifetime, ours and His. *Rejoice!*

Receiving and Giving

In the sixth month, God sent the angel Gabriel to Nazareth, a town in Galilee, to a virgin pledged to be married to a man named Joseph, a descendant of David. The virgin's name was Mary. The angel went to her and said, "Greetings, you who are highly favored! The Lord is with you." Mary was greatly troubled at his words and wondered what kind of greeting this might be. But the angel said to her, "Do not be afraid, Mary, you have found favor with God. You will be with child and give birth to a son, and you are to give him the name Jesus."

LUKE 1:26–31 NIV

God gave His gift of pure love by allowing one of us to carry out His plan. Yes, Mary's character was impeccable and her willingness to serve greatly honorable, but perhaps what God saw most when He looked at His "highly favored" daughter was the depth of her love, pure as God's and out there for everyone to see. She chose to give the gift that only she could—bearing our Savior.

At Christmas and always, we learn from Mary how to live out loud our love for God. We can grab on to whatever God places before us and live a life that says, "God gives, I receive, and then I give back. Watch!"

Today we can touch our family members, friends, and even strangers with the simple and pure love of Christ. We can do what Mary did—trust that God has found something favorable within us that fits the special work He has for us. And because He loves with a pure love that supplies whatever we lack, we can live our love for Him out loud simply by doing what He asks. That's a gift we both receive from God and can return to Him at will and without fear. Because God still gives and receives, so can we.

Activity

Help your children understand how simple loving God is—receiving His grace, following Him, and showing Him to others. As a family, decorate a greeting card for a faraway friend or put together a basket of candy for a lonely neighbor. Younger children may enjoy calling a family member on the phone and singing a carol. Remind your children that God is especially pleased when we love Him by loving others.

Truly He taught us to love one another;
His law is love and His gospel is peace.

Prayer

Father, thank You for the opportunity to follow
Mary's example and love You out loud
to those around us.

A Crown for Jesus

"He will be great and will be called the Son of the Most High; and the Lord God will give Him the throne of His father David; and He will reign over the house of Jacob forever, and His kingdom will have no end."
LUKE 1:32–33 NASB

Jesus, who always was and always will be, makes His debut in human form one holy night—and the world is forever changed. The Babe born to live and die and live again is the ultimate circle, and His divinity and sovereignty reign forever in our hearts and in our world.

Christmas reminds us again of His eternal love and unshakable grasp on our lives. Gabriel was clear in His announcement so that we can be clear in our understanding—as constant as God's breath on the leaves of the trees and steady as His hand shoving waves to the shore, Jesus' living presence encircles us and makes Christmas live eternally in our hearts.

Part of our Christmas joy, and our every-other-day joy, too, comes in partnering with Jesus in His reign. He leads and we follow, to touch those we meet with a hand of friendship, a gift of forgiveness, the grace of understanding.

He is Son of the Most High—and because of His love, we become part of His kingdom. Because of His will, we become part of His reach to those around us. Before He was born of flesh, God knew Jesus would meet our needs—and with Him we'll serve others, doing all we can to be the physical evidence of His unbroken love. It's our honor to share the gift of Christmas every day, never ending.

Activity

Make a crown with your children out of construction paper, craft sticks, pipe cleaners, or whatever you have. Use it for a tree topper, a table centerpiece, or package decoration. Explain to your children that Jesus' love is like the circle of a crown—no beginning and no end because it always was and always will be. His love and power last forever because God made Him that way.

Silent night, holy night,
Son of God, love's pure light;
Radiant beams from Thy holy face
With the dawn of redeeming grace,
Jesus, Lord at Thy birth,
Jesus, Lord at Thy birth.

Prayer

Father, thank You for King Jesus who reigns over our whole world and our family, now and forever, and lets us serve with Him.

Who Do You Trust?

This is how the birth of Jesus Christ came about: His mother Mary was pledged to be married to Joseph, but before they came together, she was found to be with child through the Holy Spirit. Because Joseph her husband was a righteous man and did not want to expose her to public disgrace, he had in mind to divorce her quietly.

MATTHEW 1:18–19 NIV

We can understand Joseph's concern, surprised by Mary's news of the Christ child's coming. Those around him might not believe Mary about her visit from the angel, and the best choice might seem to leave her quietly without facing the public doubt about the impending birth. But Joseph wasn't sure. . . .

Sometimes we're faced with situations that pit us against what we believe and what the world might believe about us. That's when we remember the value of those who have always been honest with us and the value of our own honesty, too.

Mary's character made her a credible source of information. It's important that we work to build that same credibility with those around us every day. We do that by telling the truth, by being a good representative of Christ in all we do, by following through on our promises to those we love.

Family members learn to trust each other and friends learn to trust friends over time—it's a deeply satisfying gift from God. And we learn to be trustworthy because Jesus showed us how. He has never lied to us, abandoned us, tricked us, or led us the wrong way. Let us always value our trusted relationships and work every day to make them even better, especially at Christmas.

Activity

Show your children several sets of two photos, one of a parent and one of a stranger, then one of a grandparent and one of a stranger, etc. Ask which person in each set of photos they would trust. Then do a simple exercise, such as close your eyes and tell a child that you trust him or her to give you a kiss on the cheek and explain that by being trustworthy in small areas, we gain trustworthiness in bigger ones.

In his master's steps he trod,
where the snow lay dinted;
Heat was in the very sod
which the saint had printed.

Prayer

Father, thank You for the gift of trust to share with each other and Christ. Please help us live all our relationships in trust.

His Faithful Guidance

But after he had considered this, an angel of the Lord appeared to him in a dream and said, "Joseph son of David, do not be afraid to take Mary home as your wife, because what is conceived in her is from the Holy Spirit. She will give birth to a son, and you are to give him the name Jesus, because he will save his people from their sins."
MATTHEW 1:20–21 NIV

Eager to help Joseph make his decision about marrying Mary, God chose to reveal His will in a dream. He may lead us the same way today—or, more often, He'll guide us with His word, the teachings of Jesus, and the blessing of wisdom we acquire the more we learn about Him. It's His beautiful and strong gift of guidance that grows the more we rely on it. Faithful as the earth's travels, God continues to reveal Himself to us through the simple and, especially, the scary times of our lives—allowing us to know Him better so that we'll hear His voice and learn to trust His will more securely every day, even without an angel in a dream. God showed us how Joseph trusted and followed Him so that we can, too.

May we always remember the gift of Christ, God's guiding Word come to life. May we study and cherish God's Word and humbly accept His guidance so that we'll know when

He speaks to us. Trusting the Giver to impart to us no less than the best answer and the best route, we can put our feet in the prints He leaves in every moment and mix-up in our lives. We can go on to our great and unique purposes when we go with God. Christmas is our time to begin, or begin again, our reliance on this special gift of His guidance.

Activity

For your family Bible or each child's Bible, make covers that say something like "Our Answers" or "The Gift of Guidance" and reinforce to your children how God's Word and the teachings of Jesus will always lead them and help them make good choices. Decorate the covers and place the Bibles under your Christmas tree or in another place of honor for the season.

Oh, when I was a seeker,
I sought both night and day,
I sought the Lord to help me,
And He showed me the way.

Prayer

Father, thank You for guiding us and helping us trust
You as Joseph did.

We Don't Have to Wait

For to us a child is born, to us a son is given, and the government will be on his shoulders. And he will be called Wonderful Counselor, Mighty God, Everlasting Father, Prince of Peace.

ISAIAH 9:6 NIV

Isaiah prophesied years before Jesus' physical birth, centuries before mere mortals could touch Him and see Him, millennia before our own Christmas celebrations—and it's all come true. From His detoured birth in a barn, He had all He needed to be all we need today. From the heavens themselves leading the way to the King, the love of a Savior guides us in our hearts today.

Before computers could read and microwaves could cook, He was. And He always will be. That reminder comes again at Christmas each year—and when the security in our lives can feel as transient as a stock market's gains, the promise of His everlasting being is reassurance we grab on to and don't let go.

The Everlasting Father who lives in our hearts takes on the fears and trials of this life that only feel everlasting—the jagged struggles that bounce off our raw and bleeding hearts and threaten to knock us down, shatter our focus, and leave us whimpering and beat. But unlike Isaiah's listeners, we don't have to wait for our Wonderful Counselor to appear. He came to earth with Christmas and stays to love us always.

We trust Jesus is alive in our hearts, we see Him in the kindness of strangers, and we feel Him in the love of our family members. He is everywhere at once because we all need Him, and Christmas reminds us again that our Jesus will outlast everything—and knowing that, we know all we need to know.

Activity

Help your children understand the difference between things that are everlasting and things that aren't. Let each child name something that doesn't last—a movie, a tummy ache, a birthday cake, a flower, a scratch or bruise—these aren't everlasting. But a parent's love and our Father's love are, and no matter what, no matter where, Jesus lives and loves us forever.

O come, O come, Emmanuel,
And ransom captive Israel,
That mourns in lonely exile here
Until the Son of God appear.

Prayer

Father, thank You for our everlasting Jesus and His love and grace that never end.

Present, Now and Forever

So all this was done that it might be fulfilled which was spoken by the Lord through the prophet, saying: "Behold, the virgin shall be with child, and bear a Son, and they shall call His name Immanuel," which is translated, "God with us."

MATTHEW 1:22–23 NKJV

If God is with us in Jesus (and He is), then it follows that we're with Him. Let us not overlook His beautiful and generous gift of abiding with us, so much more than sharing the same space. God's gift of abiding means sharing our lives and making us a vessel to receive and pass on His grace and peace and courage and wisdom and love. It means we can be more like Him every day because He gives us Himself.

Our Father knows our flaws and shortcomings, but He loves us more than we can mess up. And so each Christmas we're reminded of His ability to do anything but turn away from us. We joyously celebrate our "God with us" Savior's birth because the gift never ends.

Though steady stars may be obscured by passing clouds, they are no less present and powerful. And even when we feel momentarily alone and alarmed by passing fears, our Immanuel gift is no less present and powerful. Christmas tells us that from one silent night to a forever future, we abide with the One who came for us and will not leave. And close in heart, we learn to be like Him, sharing grace and peace and courage and wisdom and love because He first gave it all to us.

Activity

For each family member, draw and cut out a small heart from construction paper or a greeting card. Write on each one "God is with me" or "My Immanuel gift" or something similar. Be sure family members will have their hearts with them each day, in a wallet, lunchbox, favorite book, or other item. Remind your children that Jesus is always with them and Christmas is a beautiful time to remember and celebrate that gift of abiding even more.

O holy Child of Bethlehem,
descend to us, we pray;
Cast out our sin, and enter in,
be born in us today.
We hear the Christmas angels
the great glad tidings tell;
O come to us, abide with us, our Lord Emmanuel!

Prayer

Father, thank You for Your greatest Gift, our Savior Jesus Christ, who abides with us, and please help us be more like You in every way, every day.

Active Rest

"For nothing will be impossible with God."
LUKE 1:37 NASB

The angel Gabriel reassures Mary that what appears quite impossible to her is simply a matter of will for God. And the reassurance continues for us today, because when we practice our trust, we can make Gabriel's statement ourselves in total confidence and rest. And that rest is a wonderful gift from God.

The gift of rest comes when we trust what we can't see because we trust that He sees us, and that's enough. And if that's true and possible, no confines will ever hold His will. We trust unseen and believe the Immanuel promise of "God with us"—the most important and impossible-looking blessing of all, that gives us rest like nothing else.

But this rest is no lazy or bored time of inactivity—no, it's just the opposite, because it means we're able to enjoy our lives and our families and all God's planned for us because we trust God has everything in His hands and knows exactly what He's doing with it all and with us every minute. We can dare to dream great dreams and follow the directions He gives us. We can do our part like Mary did and leave everything else to Him—and worry not one bit but rest instead, knowing our Father is in control, seeing all we can't and seeing us without fail. It's Christmas every day.

Activity

Help your children understand God's unlimited possibilities. Can you see inside a Christmas present? No, but God can. Can you listen to everyone's prayers at one time? No, but God can. Encourage your children to give their own examples of something they or a family member can't do but God can.

Hark, hark, the wise eternal Word,
Like a weak infant cries!
In form of servant is the Lord,
And God in cradles lies.

This wonder struck the world amazed,
It shook the starry frame;
Squadrons of spirits stood and gazed,
Then down in troops they came.

Prayer

Father, thank You for the opportunity to rest in our trust of Jesus who is always able to do the impossible because of who He is.

Worshipful Serving

And Mary said: "My soul glorifies the Lord and my spirit rejoices in God my Savior, for he has been mindful of the humble state of his servant. From now on all generations will call me blessed, for the Mighty One has done great things for me—holy is his name."
LUKE 1:46–49 NIV

When we think of Mary, we think of God's perfect choice to bring human Jesus into this world, of the best mother to raise a young Savior. And we're right, but Mary's own words tell us she saw her role in a different light. She lived to serve her God, and in that way, we can all be just like her.

We can remember Mary's choice when our own work seems hard, and we can look at all we do as a beautiful chance to serve in the way God's chosen. None of us has Mary's responsibility, but each member of your family has a life equally set aside by God to serve His purposes. We can trust that God's given us each a game plan as surely as we can trust He selected Mary. And we can meet Him right there in the manger, just as she did.

Every choice we make to serve today leads us to more opportunity tomorrow. It's a gift He's given us—to be able to partner with Him and make a difference in the lives of those around us.

In your home, caring for each other and loving and helping each other serves God. In your community, telling others about our Savior and sharing what you have with them serves God. Every act small or large that shows God to someone else is an act of worship. It's God's gift we have the pleasure of giving away again and again, Christmas Day and every day.

Activity

Choose a service you can do as a family, perhaps invite a new neighbor for a meal or help a relative with shopping or cleaning. Talk to your children as you work about Jesus and how we're worshipping Him and serving Him when we reach out to others in help or support, and that's a gift to Him from us!

Therefore, Christian men, be sure,
wealth or rank possessing,
You who now will bless the poor
shall yourselves find blessing.

Prayer

Father, thank You for giving us so many opportunities to worship You by serving You. Please show us how to serve You today.

Prepared and Ready

In those days Caesar Augustus issued a decree that a census should be taken of the entire Roman world. (This was the first census that took place while Quirinius was governor of Syria.) And everyone went to his own town to register.
LUKE 2:1–3 NIV

Hundreds of years before Christ's human birth, God prepared the world for Him and prepared the way for His earthly parents to arrive in the little town of Bethlehem. God continues to prepare today for us, because He's in everything we do. Sometimes we see, and sometimes we don't.

Even when we don't understand a situation or see how something routine or unremarkable could be God's work, we can pay attention and open ourselves up to His guidance by taking nothing for granted, by serving with a willing heart.

Time spent with family and friends is preparation for something wonderful. Kindness to strangers and patience in difficulty is preparation for something wonderful. Private, quiet time listening to God and learning about Him is preparation for something wonderful. Christmas reminds us of His attention to detail and long-range planning, and He's granted us the gift of being part of His work that still goes on today.

We all have many "Bethlehems" we're headed to in our lives, and God will see that we're prepared when we get there. He will prepare the way and prepare us for the way. Jesus' carefully planned birth reminds us of that, and His life enables us to be part of all that's to come.

Activity

At the census in Bethlehem, Mary and Joseph and the other people were counted. Help your children count something else—days. On your family calendar or a big, colorful calendar just for the kids, on each day starting today, draw a heart or a cross and tell your children that that symbol will remind all of you to pray every day to be prepared for God's will. Pray as a family and encourage your children to say their private prayers, too.

O little town of Bethlehem,
how still we see thee lie!
Above thy deep and dreamless sleep
the silent stars go by.
Yet in thy dark streets shineth
the everlasting Light;
The hopes and fears of all the years
are met in thee tonight.

Prayer

Father, thank You for the gift of Your divine preparation and please help us prepare for all You've planned for our family today and always.

Home and Home Again

*So Joseph also went up from the town of Nazareth in Galilee to Judea,
to Bethlehem the town of David, because he belonged to the house and
line of David. He went there to register with Mary, who was pledged
to be married to him and was expecting a child.*

LUKE 2:4–5 NIV

The journey Joseph and Mary would take to the delivery room God had chosen was a journey back to their homeland, back to where their story began and a long-passed-on prophet knew:

Out of [Bethlehem] will come for me one who will be ruler over Israel, whose origins are from of old, from ancient times.
MICAH 5:2 NIV

"Home" is where we meet God, where we have Christmas every day, where we rest knowing God is in charge and we don't have to be. Coming home to our families each night brings us joy and peace, and working through our days to get home to God every second allows so much more.

It's a lifelong journey for us, and we meet God on the way time after time. We meet Him in the blessings He showers on us, in the friends who help and support us, in the family members who love us and journey with us. And we keep going, because no matter how scared we might get at some intersections or unknown roads, we know God is waiting, holding arms open wide to welcome us in, so glad to be with us even if we get a little lost or sidetracked along the way.

God knows our steps, and when we trust them to Him, we, like Mary and Joseph, will find safe passage and the delivery room for all we've been created to bring forth, too. We can trust Jesus to be there, as home and home again we go.

Activity

Have mom or dad promise each child they'll be somewhere with a big hug when the child finds them. Then have one parent or an older child walk each child a long and winding route through the house or yard to get to the other parent. When the child arrives, have the parent keep his or her promise.

"Joseph dearest, Joseph mine,
Help me cradle the Child divine;
God reward thee and all that's thine
In paradise," so prays the mother Mary.

"Gladly, dear one, lady mine,
Help I cradle this child of thine;
God's own light on us both shall shine
In paradise, as prays the mother Mary."

Prayer

Father, thank You for always planning the perfect journey for us. Help us trust You and follow You unafraid.

Chosen Today

*"I am the LORD your God, who teaches you what is best for you,
who directs you in the way you should go."*
ISAIAH 48:17 NIV

Mary's donkey was sure-footed and stable, just the right creature for the job of transporting our Savior and His mother. God chose the destination and the route—and He also chose the method to accomplish this most important goal, and He's still doing that in our lives today.

God chooses the family to give us and the abilities and talents and gifts to give each one of us. At Christmas, we may tend to focus on the tangible gifts we give others and the gifts of love and grace God has given us in Jesus. We also want to remember all the other gifts He's given us so that we can play our parts in His continually unfolding story starring Jesus.

God has many jobs to get done, and getting Mary safely to Bethlehem was one of them, so He chose the right donkey from among all the other donkeys in the world. Today, He chooses you and your family members from all the other people in the world to do the jobs only you can do. He knows what we're all best at, and He gives us the opportunity to experience that great joy of working with Him to accomplish His goals.

God trusts us completely with the jobs He's set aside for us. As we keep His destination and route in mind, we learn how to be the vehicle to help others, show them who God is, introduce them to Jesus, and be their friend along the way.

Activity

Give each child a simple destination (another room), a simple route (around the corner), and ask him or her to be the method to deliver something there: Have a child carry a love note or tiny gift to another family member in the other room. Explain that's how God works with us—giving us a job to share Him with others however we can.

Jesus, our Brother, strong and good,
Was humbly born in a stable rude,
And the friendly beasts around Him stood,
Jesus, our Brother, strong and good.

"I," said the donkey, shaggy and brown,
"I carried His mother uphill and down,
I carried His mother to Bethlehem town;
I," said the donkey, shaggy and brown.

Prayer

Father, thank You for giving us jobs as important as You gave the donkey carrying Mary and Jesus, and please help us do what we do best for You.

Promises Now and Forever

"Your house and your kingdom shall endure before Me forever;
your throne shall be established forever."
2 SAMUEL 7:16 NASB

When God made that promise, how must David have felt? Was he secure enough in God's love and faithfulness that he believed Him? We believe he was because we know that he followed through on his work for God and rarely failed to seek God's grace. And today, we remember God's promises of old that apply to us.

Christmas reminds us of the best promise ever made and kept. And Jesus learned well from His Father. His word to be with us always (Matthew 28:20) and His words of peace (Matthew 11:28) and rest (John 14:27) and victory (John 16:33) comfort us when times are hard and embolden us when work awaits. And perhaps Jesus modeled those promises for us so that we could follow.

No matter what, no matter when, no matter where—you can faithfully promise your family members to be with them in their hearts, to support them up close or far away, to remain loyal and trusting forevermore. You can promise to be a sanctuary, a safe place, a comfort zone they can always find. You can make these promises because God and Jesus make and keep Their promises and will help you keep yours. It's a gift of follow-through we experience the more we lean on Their promises and claim those promises for ourselves.

Children will come to learn that some promises, like God's promise of Jesus, take a long time to come to pass, but that doesn't make them any less true. Our promises are only to be made with great thought and sincere intentions, so let God's track record guide us at Christmas and always.

Activity

Have each family member write or draw a picture of a promise to another family member—for example, a young child can promise a hug for mom or dad. Put each promise in an envelope or small box and place it under your Christmas tree. Open the promises Christmas Eve and have each family member follow through.

O come, Thou Day-spring, come and cheer
Our spirits by Thine advent here;
Disperse the gloomy clouds of night,
And death's dark shadows put to flight.
Rejoice! Rejoice! Emmanuel
Shall come to thee, O Israel.

Prayer

Father, thank You for Your promises that always come to life, and for Christmas when we celebrate the greatest promise of all.

Knowing What's Important

And she brought forth her firstborn Son, and wrapped Him in swaddling cloths, and laid Him in a manger, because there was no room for them in the inn.

LUKE 2:7 NKJV

We would imagine that, after a long journey and when about to deliver the world's Savior, Mary and Joseph were exhausted yet excited, eager to get to a comfortable resting place. They couldn't phone ahead for reservations or check online for vacancies, but they must have expected to find at least an indoor room and basic necessities.

Perhaps they were scared when there was no place to stay and no bed for Mary and the Baby. Perhaps they were confused, wondering why God wouldn't provide for them what they needed to serve in this very special way. Or perhaps they trusted that He was providing. Perhaps they trusted that He had not forgotten about their most important mission. Perhaps they trusted each step that led them to the manger.

Christmas reminds us to trust God's sovereign plan even if we get scared or confused. Christmas reminds us that God's methods may seem unusual sometimes, and we may not understand every turn or development, but He is always in control.

He showed us His perfect attention to detail and planning when He chose the place for His most important gift. And He left everything less important somewhere else. That's a guide we can use—the best choice is always to follow God and let everything else less important settle somewhere else. Christmas is a beautiful celebration of Mary and Joseph's trust, and that's a gift they still give to us today.

Activity

Get an empty first-aid kit and let your children put silly things in the box—toys, spoons, crayons, anything that would be useless for first aid. Help them see that something full of the less important stuff isn't what we need, and the inn was full of everything less important than Jesus, so Mary and Joseph didn't need it—they only needed to trust and follow God.

Away with our fears!
The Godhead appears
In Christ reconciled
The Father of mercies in Jesus the Child.

He comes from above,
In manifest love,
Desire of our eyes,
The meek Lamb of God,
in a manger He lies.

Prayer

Father, thank You for always having the perfect plan for Your will and for helping us know what we need to know to do our most important work.

A Manger Spoken For

So it was, that while they were there, the days were completed for her to be delivered. And she brought forth her firstborn Son, and wrapped Him in swaddling cloths, and laid Him in a manger, because there was no room for them in the inn.

Luke 2:6–7 nkjv

We might read that part of the Christmas story and wonder how that no-vacancy detail could have escaped God's attention. How could He have failed to make room at the inn for His Son and His family? But look again, and we'll see something else.

That manger wasn't an afterthought or backup plan if something else didn't work out. It was a gift, a tangible demonstration of God's focus and order, because there was room for only one Savior. And the gift from old is re-created each day in our hearts where, again, there is room for only one Savior.

Is your heart running low on peace or joy, trust or belief or eagerness to live your life? Whatever your heart needs is wrapped perfectly in the gift of the living Christ—joy to the world at His birth and right now, too.

And as surely as He filled that manger designed only for Him, He fills your heart with the grace and will and power you need to live the life He's designed only for you, because you are no afterthought or backup plan either.

Because He is our greatest teacher and example, we learn to live this beautiful life as we make room in the manger of our hearts for the peace and joy He's created especially for us. And Christmas is a wonderful time to begin.

Activity

Look at as many pictures as you can find of nativity scenes: in books, on the computer, on greeting cards. Gather any nativity scenes you have, perhaps even unveil a new one for your family, or draw or make a simple one together. Ask your children how many Saviors are in each nativity. The answer is always one—the One God sent because there could be no other. Remind your children how special and unique Jesus is and how our hearts are designed to hold only Him.

Joy to the world! The Lord is come!
Let earth receive her King;
Let ev'ry heart prepare Him room,
And heaven and nature sing.

Prayer

Father, thank You for the manger You planned and our Jesus to fill it and for our family and our Jesus to fill our hearts.

Wrapped in Focus

And she brought forth her firstborn Son, and wrapped Him in swaddling cloths, and laid Him in a manger, because there was no room for them in the inn.
LUKE 2:7 NKJV

When Jesus Son of Man (John 3:13) was baby Jesus in the manger, He was truly one of us, needing a loving mother's tender care—and Mary met His needs, wrapping Him in cloths warm and soft, holding Him close, cradling the head He couldn't yet hold up, measuring her breath to His. In the very beginning, life for our Savior was simple.

And Jesus Son of God (John 11:27) has been meeting our needs ever since, at the beginning, middle, or end of anything. He wraps us in His love, cradles our fearful and hurting hearts, and measures out the grace we need to carry on. It's a gift of *focus* on us as if we're all He has to tend to, the only needy baby in the house.

Before Jesus was brought physically into our world, the believers in God accessed Him through the priests at the temple in formal ways. God's love for them was no less strong than His love for us, but God's greatest Gift to us changed forever our interaction with Him. Jesus is *our* Most Holy Place, and He lives in us every minute, completely accessible, completely focused on us.

We can trust Him to respond to our every cry the way Mary responded to Jesus' baby whimpers, His childhood hurts—the human side of His world. He knows well how important to us fragile and insecure sheep a close and powerful Shepherd is. He knows and He responds, with guidance and peace, the Son of God close as man needs, Christmas alive every moment.

Activity

Gather some strips of cloth, towels, or old clothing. Hold your children close and gently wrap the cloths around them and say with each wrap something like, "Jesus brings His love, Jesus brings His peace, Jesus is listening to you." And tell them that His focus on them is just as secure as your arms around them right now.

Away in a manger, no crib for a bed,
The little Lord Jesus laid down
his sweet head.
The stars in the bright sky looked
down where he lay,
The little Lord Jesus asleep on the hay.

Prayer

Father, thank You for Jesus' human birth and life and His wonderful ability to know just what we need.

Shepherding Us Now

And there were shepherds living out in the fields nearby,
keeping watch over their flocks at night.
LUKE 2:8 NIV

The shepherds in the fields seem unlikely representatives of
our Lord; but it's no mistake, because we are so much like the
wayward sheep they tended. And knowing our every need, God
sent us a Shepherd.

One special and sparkly time of the year, we remember God's
gift to our world, but let us not forget that the Jesus sent for
the whole world was sent so that you and I and our families
would each know Him personally. Just like the caring and
watchful shepherd knows every sheep, Jesus knows each
of us inside and out, our needs and weaknesses, so He,
too, keeps watch over His flock, day and night.

The sheep in the field can't get where they're
going on their own. They don't know where the
best grazing fields are, where the fresh streams
of water are, how to fight off predators or
battle the elements. But their shepherd does.
And he stays with them, nearby, guiding and
protecting. That's why the comparison
between the shepherd of the field and the
Shepherd of our lives is right as a star
atop your tree.

We, too, can't get by on our

own; and because of Jesus, we don't have to. He will stay with us, nearby, guiding and protecting us. He will show us where our life's work is and then walk with us every step. And if we'll continue to be like the shepherd's sheep and trust the shepherd—our Shepherd—we'll know the unending celebration of Christmas as we journey through all the fields of our lives.

Activity

Have each child make or draw a candy cane or use a real (wrapped) one. Tell your children that the cane represents Jesus the Shepherd who always watches over us. Place each candy cane near each child's bed or affix it to the door as a reminder that Jesus is closer than a thought and can always be trusted to guide and protect us.

The first Noel the angel did say
Was to certain poor shepherds in fields as they lay;
In fields where they lay keeping their sheep,
On a cold winter's night that was so deep.
Noel, Noel, Noel, Noel,
Born is the King of Israel.

Prayer

Father, thank You for Jesus' understanding of our sheeplike ways and for being the Shepherd we need every day.

Unafraid

And behold, an angel of the Lord stood before them, and the glory of the Lord shone around them, and they were greatly afraid.
Luke 2:9 NKJV

Unaware of when or how the Savior Jesus would arrive in their world, the shepherds waited. Then when He was born, the "glory of the Lord" around them was all they could see, and they were frightened and confused. Sometimes our fears become all we can see, but God is bigger. And with Jesus's birth, God gives us the gift of possibility—the unfolding of something wonderful in every situation, even the frightening ones.

Whenever we're scared, we need to remember that God is there, no matter what we see. His glory is on us, waiting to shine through us for others to see.

We always have the possibility of discovering and creating great things from whatever happens—because Jesus is steadying us in our fears so that we can see what to do next. No matter what the experience, the place to look for help is always in our hearts where Jesus lives.

We can think of our fear as one big bubble around us and then picture it full of Jesus. He smiles at us and holds us close so that all the fear seeps out like air from a tiny hole in a tricycle tire. Then when we're calm and secure in His presence, we're able to see the possibility of everything remaining—the possibility of learning more about His love and our purpose here, of being more a part of how He touches those around us.

It's a possibility we don't want to miss out of fear, and Jesus says we never have to.

Activity

Turn off all the lights so that your family members are unable to see each other (take care younger ones aren't upset). Then light a candle and see how quickly everyone's faces come into view, hidden by the darkness but there all along. Explain to your children that Jesus fills up the scared spaces in us just like the candlelight fills up the darkness, and because of Him so near, great joys await.

While shepherds watched their flocks by night,
All seated on the ground,
The angel of the Lord came down,
And glory shone around.

Prayer

Lord, thank You for removing our fears as Jesus pushes them away and helps us see what He'll do next in our lives.

Just for You

But the angel said to them, "Do not be afraid; for behold, I bring you good news of great joy which will be for all the people; for today in the city of David there has been born for you a Savior, who is Christ the Lord."
Luke 2:10–11 NASB

The angel reassured the shepherds that their Savior had come, for them, for each of them and just as sure, He came for us, for each of us. The Christ Child King already knew each of those shepherds' hearts and souls and how they would go on to bring glory to Him—and He was prepared to give them what they needed.

Since that Christmas morning, His knowing and giving continues. For every one of us who waits in the pastures or classrooms or workplaces of our lives and needs our Savior close, He came.

He came with big plans, too, plans for us and our families because we are all special, unique, and deeply loved children of God. The shepherds received a personal announcement of His arrival, and each Christmas morning is ours.

Like a beautifully wrapped present for each of us as big as the whole world, He holds great wonders yet unseen; and because of Him and His grace, we can become what He already sees: disciples like the shepherds with important work to do. And Jesus joys in that, in each one of us able to do our specific job for Him, that He's already chosen. It's a gift of His intimacy for each of us.

Activity

Make a simple birth announcement for Jesus out of construction paper, one for each family member. On the inside, note Jesus' name, place of birth, and the reason (God loves me). On the outside of each announcement, write a family member's name because Jesus came for each one of us. Remind your children how special they all are and how Jesus will use their lives to do amazing things only they can do.

It came upon the midnight clear,
That glorious song of old,
From angels bending near the earth,
To touch their harps of gold;
"Peace on the earth, good will to men,
From Heaven's all gracious King!"
The world in solemn stillness lay,
To hear the angels sing.

Prayer

Father, thank You for sending Jesus for each of us,
and for helping us become what He already sees.

Signs Everywhere

"And this will be the sign to you: You will find a Babe wrapped in swaddling cloths, lying in a manger."
LUKE 2:12 NKJV

The sweet, tiny Babe who made His human entry into our world was long awaited and gladly welcomed. He was a breathing, growing, smiling sign of God's love for all who would receive Him. A Child born amid the animals bore our salvation, the newborn sign we celebrate at Christmas and the never-ending sign we lean on every day.

But God wasn't done. He sends us other signs today, signs to guide, equip, inspire, and support us and our families in everything we do.

We have a sign of God's grace in the loving people who forgive us and help us when we fail. We have a sign of His faith in us in the second, third, or seventy-third chance He gives us to follow His will. We have a sign of His delight in us in the joys we experience in our lives—including our family time at Christmas and beyond.

When we pay attention to God's signs, we'll be as amazed as the shepherds, blown away but steadied to the core by His limitless generosity and unfailing ability to speak to us and give to us what we need. Let's keep looking.

And let's also take note of the opportunities to be a sign of God's love to those around us, at home, school, work, and play. Encouragement, support, forgiveness, courage, understanding— every good and God-inspired gift we give is a sign of Him to those who need Him. Let's keep looking.

Christmas, past or beyond, the signs just keep coming. Gifts abound.

Activity

Create a private "sign" for your family that means "I love you," something such as a tug on the ear, fingers crossed, or something the children choose. Help your children make the sign to their other parent, and begin and end each day with it, reminding them of God's signs of love everywhere. Keep looking!

"To you, in David's town, this day
Is born of David's line
The Savior, who is Christ the Lord,
And this shall be the sign,
And this shall be the sign.

The heav'nly Babe you there shall find
To human view displayed,
All meanly wrapped in swathing bands,
And in a manger laid,
And in a manger laid."

Prayer

*Father, thank You for Your signs and the chance to be one,
and please help us not to miss any.*

Cattle Lowing, Us Loving

You will go out in joy and be led forth in peace; the mountains and hills will burst into song before you, and all the trees of the field will clap their hands.

Isaiah 55:12 niv

God made each of us unique, one-of-a-kind, in this big, full world. He knows each one of us by every little thing we do and every thought and dream we have. God's gift of individuality, of one-of-a-kind-ness allows each of us to worship and serve in the way we know best.

Babies are often comforted by the low, steady sounds of animals, and those surrounding baby Jesus did their part to celebrate His physical entry into our world. "The cattle are lowing, the baby awakes, But little Lord Jesus, no crying he makes. . . ." Not able to speak of course, but able to honor Him just the same, the animals did what they could with what they had, each one doing his best. That's all God asks of us.

Each decision we make to praise God and tell Jesus's story in the way only we can is the perfect use of our gift of individuality, our one-of-a-kind-ness. God only asks that we love our Savior nonstop and never feel our efforts are less than anyone else's. Everything we do to honor Jesus, when it comes from our heart and is the best we can offer, says, "I love You" to Him, and that's always right.

Christmas is a time to remember that Jesus is One, but He's able to speak to each of us—and hear each of us—in the best way for each of us. May our celebrations today be a comfort to Him as the animals in the stable were that beautiful morning.

Activity

Look at a family portrait or snapshot, and appreciate the differences among members. Allow family members to say how they would have uniquely welcomed Jesus if they'd been there with the animals. Maybe younger children will imitate the animals or draw a picture—no way is wrong as we remember that Jesus loves us each for who we are.

And then they heard the angels tell
"Who were the first to cry Nowell?
Animals all, as it befell,
In the stable where they did dwell!
Joy shall be theirs in the morning!"

Prayer

Father, thank You for understanding our words and thoughts and actions as we celebrate Jesus in our own way.

Glory, Peace, and Me

And suddenly there was with the angel a multitude of the heavenly
host praising God and saying: "Glory to God in the highest,
and on earth peace, goodwill toward men!"
Luke 2:13–14 NKJV

Glory and peace always go together. It was so since Jesus and Christmas came together so that His love and we could go together. It's a gift that gives us even more than we first see.

The gift of praising God—giving Him the glory for all we are and all we do because He makes it all possible—takes our minds off ourselves and onto God who's in charge, and that gives us peace no matter what. Christmas helps us see that connection as we celebrate Jesus' birth and all that means. Because He has come and saved us, every day and every situation is a point of praise, and peace follows.

So when we find ourselves in pain or fear, confusion or despair, we know how to get out. We turn to God, praise Him, trust Him, and rely on Him because we know we don't have to do anything by ourselves, and we breathe in peace only He can give.

And we can help our family members when they're hurting, too. We can pray with them and help them focus on the greatness and power of God. We can remember Jesus' coming into our world so that our world would never be the same. We can give thanks to God for His close and constant care and rest in His love and grace with them. We can be a bearer of peace and help them find their own.

Glory and peace always go together. The gift we give gives back even more.

Activity

As a family make up a song, something short
such as "Jesus is my Lord/Jesus loves me/So no
matter what/I am at peace." Sing the song with
your children on the way to school or daycare
or when they're getting dressed each morning.
Sing it to yourself, too!

O come, let us adore him,
O come let us adore him,
O come, let us adore him,
Christ the Lord.

Sing, choirs of angels, sing in exultation;
O sing, all ye citizens of heaven above!
Glory to God in the highest.

Prayer

Lord, thank You for Your gift of peace lived out in
Jesus and for helping us always experience Your peace
and glorify You at the same time.

Choosing to Share

So it was, when the angels had gone away from them into heaven, that the shepherds said to one another, "Let us now go to Bethlehem and see this thing that has come to pass, which the Lord has made known to us." And they came with haste and found Mary and Joseph, and the Babe lying in a manger. Now when they had seen Him, they made widely known the saying which was told them concerning this Child.
LUKE 2:15–17 NKJV

We aren't told the angels ordered the shepherds to do anything, but they decided together "let us now go. . ."; and in their excitement, they took God's gift of choice and saw their joy ripple far and wide.

We have the same gift of choice today and so very much to share. We can make "widely known" what Jesus has brought to our hearts, first among our families, and then as we reach way, way out, as wide as the sky, as deep as a hug, as pure as understanding, to all those we meet.

God doesn't give us an order or make Christmas come only if we contact ten people and tell them the story. Instead, He chooses to trust us with His gift of choice, to give us all we need to know about Jesus to share Him with someone else—that

He is our Savior and He loves us all.

That we get to live that great news every day is a blessing God willingly pours on us—telling others about it is a choice we make to be a blessing to them. God's plan lets us be a part.

Activity

Have each family member choose something they like (candy, favorite toy, cherished book) and tell other family members about it, because we bring joy to others when we share what we know. Have one parent pretend not to know Jesus and have the other parent or an older child explain Christmas.

"Fear not, then," said the angel, "Let nothing you affright,
This day is born a Savior of a pure Virgin bright,
To free all those who trust in Him
from Satan's power and might."

The shepherds at those tidings rejoiced much in mind,
And left their flocks a-feeding in tempest, storm, and wind,
And went to Bethl'em straightaway
this blessed Babe to find.

Prayer

Father, thank You for trusting us with the gift of choice, for allowing us to be part of Jesus' story by telling others about Him.

Time Well Spent

And all who heard it were amazed at what the shepherds said to them.
But Mary treasured up all these things and pondered them in her heart.
Luke 2:18–19 NIV

Like an election or a hurricane, Jesus must have been the talk of the fields and streets as more and more people heard about His arrival. Did they want to journey to see Him? Did they have questions for His earthly parents? How did Joseph and Mary handle those who wanted to worship their Babe?

We know Mary wanted time alone with her Father. And because we so often need the same thing, God grants us His gift of solitude—time alone with Him because He wants time alone with each of us.

The gift of solitude and special time with God as if you're the only person in the world blesses you and pleases Him. Yes, the Christmas season brings activities and parties and fun times with family and friends, but let's not neglect this special gift because it's one of God's favorites, when He gets to spend uninterrupted time with us, talking, listening, quiet.

Jesus was human and understood this need and frequently left His disciples and went away to pray to His Father alone, and He was always strengthened afterward. When we claim God's gift of solitude with Him and take time away to pray, we're strengthened, too, renewed and reignited.

Taking time to "ponder"—to talk and listen to God—will help us learn from the past and plan for the future. God still makes time for all His children, so let's all make time for Him, at Christmas and always.

Activity

Make each family member a little four-page storybook to look at in private time with God—just pieces of construction paper, canvas, or even cut up paper plates stapled together. Pages can be simple drawings, favorite Bible verses, pictures cut from magazines or newspapers, blank pages for adults, or prayers written for little ones.

How silently, how silently, the wondrous Gift is giv'n;
So God imparts to human hearts
the blessings of His Heav'n.
No ear may hear His coming, but in this world of sin,
Where meek souls will receive Him, still,
the dear Christ enters in.

Prayer

Father, thank You for the private world we share with You,
for Jesus who made it possible at Christmas and always.

"This Way"

Now after Jesus was born in Bethlehem of Judea in the days of Herod the king, behold, wise men from the East came to Jerusalem, saying, "Where is He who has been born King of the Jews? For we have seen His star in the East and have come to worship Him."
Matthew 2:1–2 NKJV

When Jesus first came into our world, those who heard of His arrival had the privilege of directing others to Him. And even though He's not arriving again as a Holy Babe, people today still need help in getting to Him. And that's where we get to play a part—we have the same privilege today: the gift of directing others to Jesus.

Sometimes we'll encounter people who seem afraid to trust Jesus, but we can help them see that Jesus takes away our fears because He's bigger and more powerful than anything that could frighten us.

Sometimes we'll encounter people who seem unsure that Jesus can love them because they haven't always loved Him, but we can help them see that Jesus always loves us first and will never turn us away if we make the choice to follow Him.

Sometimes we'll encounter people who seem confused about Jesus and need to hear our story, and we can help them by telling them how everything began at Christmas and will never end because Jesus is our Savior who will never abandon us. We can direct them to Him by guiding them with our own lives, by being both an example and a road map that those who don't know Jesus can use to get to Him.

It's a beautiful gift God's given us—let's not miss an opportunity to be wise and generous with our directions.

Activity

Draw a simple, colorful map with your children, including "You are here" marked with a star, a path labeled "Jesus' Way," and then the destination labeled "Peace and Love"—because that's what traveling with Jesus gives us. Let each family member take the path on the map with a game piece or other small item. Remind your children that they're never too young to give "Jesus directions."

We three kings of Orient are;
Bearing gifts we traverse afar,
Field and fountain, moor and mountain,
Following yonder star.
O, star of wonder, star of light,
Star with royal beauty bright,
Westward leading, still proceeding,
Guide us to thy perfect light.

Prayer

Father, thank You for those around us who need directions to Jesus and the opportunity to help guide them.

Free in Surrender

When Herod the king heard this, he was troubled, and all Jerusalem with him. . . . Then Herod, when he had secretly called the wise men, determined from them what time the star appeared. And he sent them to Bethlehem and said, "Go and search carefully for the young Child, and when you have found Him, bring back word to me, that I may come and worship Him also."
MATTHEW 2:3, 7–8 NKJV

King Herod was afraid, "troubled," and threatened by what he didn't understand. Because he was afraid of having to give up his power to a superior king, he turned to a life of trickery, deceit, and suspicion, when he could've chosen to worship the Christ Child instead.

Sadly, he misunderstood Jesus' power, believing that it was power that took away from him when it's actually power that gives to us more than we can imagine. We have nothing to fear from the kind of surrender that lets Jesus rule in our hearts.

No earthly king can do what Jesus does. No earthly king can set us free when we surrender to him, but that's exactly what Jesus does. The best order for our lives is Jesus at the top, our Savior who came on Christmas to be with us forever. Surrendering to Him means simply opening our hearts so that we have Him to guide and direct us in every situation we face. And in surrendering to Him, we are free, in bondage to no one, to no ideals that are counter to our Lord's.

Families together are strong and protective, and we willingly surrender to the circle of those we love. Our surrendering to Jesus makes us strong and protected, and it's a choice we get to make and encourage others to make, too. Christmas is a great time for surrender.

Activity

Draw a basic organizational chart with a box for Jesus at the top, an arrow drawn down, and a photo or simple drawing of each family member. Explain to your children that when Jesus is in charge of our lives, we're free of worry and fear because we trust God to be in control and hold us safely in His hands.

They looked up and saw a star
Shining in the east, beyond them far;
And to the earth it gave great light,
And so it continued both day and night.

Prayer

Father, thank You for the kingdom of our hearts where Jesus rules and for the choice to surrender to You and live in peace.

Overjoyed

After they had heard the king, they went on their way, and the star they had seen in the east went ahead of them until it stopped over the place where the child was. When they saw the star, they were overjoyed.
MATTHEW 2:9–10 NIV

Perhaps Baby Jesus wasn't surprised by the "overjoyed" reaction of the wise men, because He has been doing everything for us "overwell" ever since. He overloves us, overguides us and overprotects us—and the gift we've been given of Jesus' overattention causes us to be overjoyed, too.

That's because we learn His habits and His tendency to be overpresent in our lives—present when we call His name and present when we don't even think about it. He's present because He loves us more than we know and looks out for us more closely than we can understand.

He's overinterested in everything on our minds, so no matter how small something may seem in relation to great concerns, Jesus cares and keeps His attention focused on our every thought, hurt, fear, and feeling. He understands everything we can't and sees all our situations and problems from every angle. He stands ready to help in every way we'll allow. He just can't do anything in a small way.

Christmas reminds us of the journey of the wise men to see Jesus—let it remind us of His journey to be with us, each one of us, with the overattention only He can provide.

Activity

Look at a book in the dark with a penlight—that represents often as much as we can see. Then look at the book with a spotlight or the brightest flashlight you have—that's how Jesus sees everything going on in our lives. He provides overcare for us, a gift of greater love more than we can "see" and never less than we need.

And by the light of that same star
Three Wise Men came from country far;
To seek for a King was their intent,
And to follow the star wherever it went.

This star drew nigh to the northwest,
Over Bethlehem it took its rest;
And there it did both stop and stay,
Right over the place where Jesus lay.

Prayer

Father, thank You for receiving our love and loving us back through Jesus more than we can understand.

Giving Our Best

On coming to the house, they saw the child with his mother Mary, and they bowed down and worshiped him. Then they opened their treasures and presented him with gifts of gold and of incense and of myrrh.
MATTHEW 2:11 NIV

Those men traveled full-handed to present gifts of the best their culture knew to the best gift our world would ever know. A couple thousand years later and we're still traveling to Him, bearing gifts of the best we have, and we learn that it's us—our love and devotion and faith and trust and service. Our life is the most cherished gift our Savior receives, because that's how we can be part of helping others know Him.

And the wise men showed us how—they worshipped the Lord Jesus first and then presented their gifts. They understood the first Noel and set for us and our families an example of God's wishes at Christmas and beyond: worship our Savior because He's our Savior and then honor the King with all we have to give. This order brings Christmas alive year-round because we come to see that worship is in everything we do, and giving our best is a gift that we live.

It's a never-ending Christmas celebration to represent Jesus to those around us. So when we love Him by loving others in every little or big way we know, every day of the year, He sees a birthday gift, and the joy continues.

Activity

Draw a simple picture of each family member or print a small copy from your computer. Let each person sign his photo "love, name" and roll it up like a piece of taffy. Secure the ends with Christmas ribbon and add a gift tag: "To: God. From: me." Place each rolled photo under the Christmas tree and explain to your children that the best and most lasting gift we can give God is the gift of ourselves to live for Him. When we give ourselves to Him, we allow the best life He's planned for us to come to light, starting at Christmas.

The wise may bring their learning,
the rich may bring their wealth,
And some may bring their greatness,
and some bring strength and health;
We, too, would bring our treasures to offer to the King;
We have no wealth or learning;
what shall we children bring?

We'll bring Him hearts that love Him.

Prayer

Father, thank You for the opportunity to give all we are to You, on Christmas and always, to worship You by giving to others.

Our Breathing Gift of Grace

For it is by grace you have been saved, through faith—
and this not from yourselves, it is the gift of God.
Ephesians 2:8 niv

Every year at Christmastime, we think of the New Year coming—and the chance to make it better than the last because of God's gift of grace. We'll grow as followers of Christ, grow within our families, have the opportunity to work toward new goals, accomplish much, and plan much more. The calendar keeps time, but God makes it all possible.

God's grace, breathing in Jesus, is never out of season, never out of reach. It makes our lives empty of limits and full of the best that's yet to be. Through every interaction with Jesus, with family members, with friends or with strangers, He teaches us new lessons and reteaches old ones.

He takes our mistakes and missteps and gives us new opportunities in their place so that we can accept His grace and make better choices next time. It's His love for us lived out loud in everything we do because of Jesus' coming to life in this world with us. Without our Savior, a new day or new year or new opportunity would mean nothing. Because of Him, each moment means everything.

Jesus helps us start over and make

things better whether it's the New Year or not—because we need a new beginning like the miracle of Christmas, and He says we can have it any time we humbly ask and prepare to receive. God accepts our wounded hearts and erases everything that hurts—because of the greatest Gift of our Jesus. Every year we have Christmas to remind us, and every breath we have Him close enough to tell us.

Activity

Wrap a small empty box and hang it as an ornament or place it under your tree to represent God's grace living through Jesus. The small box's emptiness that your children can't touch or photograph is like God's grace that can't be contained because it's limitless and Jesus is everywhere. Let the box be a reminder you bring out at Christmas each year.

O holy night, the stars are brightly shining;
It is the night of the dear Savior's birth!
Long lay the world in sin and error pining,
Till He appeared and the soul felt its worth.
A thrill of hope, the weary soul rejoices,
For yonder breaks a new and glorious morn.

Prayer

Father, thank You for a festive red and green reminder of Your greatest Gift every year—the greatest Gift that lasts forever.

About the Author

Karon Phillips Goodman is the author of Unafraid: Living God's Plan on a Ladder and a Promise, Pursued by the Shepherd: Every Woman's Journey from Lost to Found, *the Woman's Guide series and more. She is a popular speaker for women's events and lives in Alabama. Please contact Karon at:*

Karon Goodman
P.O. Box 83
Ashland, AL 36251
Karon@KaronGoodman.com